Exploring as You WALK IN THE CITY

Also by Phyllis S. Busch
with photographs by Mary M. Thacher

EXPLORING AS YOU WALK IN THE MEADOW
A WALK IN THE SNOW

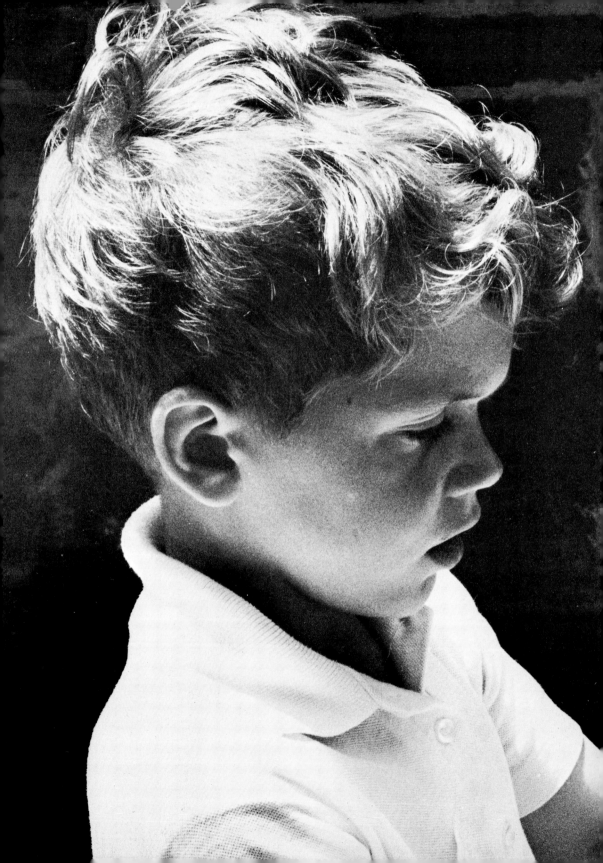

Exploring as You WALK IN THE CITY

Phyllis S. Busch

Photographed by Mary M. Thacher

J. B. Lippincott Company   Philadelphia and New York

To Lou

Enthusiastic Explorer of Cities

The photographer gratefully acknowledges the cooperation
of Jim Buck's Dogs for the photograph on page 24.

The pictures on pages 8 and 9 were photographed by Arlene Strong.

U.S. Library of Congress Cataloging in Publication Data

Busch, Phyllis S
Exploring as you walk in the city.

SUMMARY: Points out many elements in nature that the city dweller can observe
and study. "Leader's guide for Exploring as you walk in the city" ([4] p.) in pocket.
1. Natural history—Juvenile literature. [1. Natural history] I. Thacher, Mary M., illus.
II. Title.
PZ10.B94Ev   500.9'173'2   71-38942   ISBN-0-397-31223-7

A walk along a city street becomes an adventure when you are the explorer.

Your body has wonderful tools for making discoveries—
    two eyes for seeing
    and a nose for smelling
    two ears for hearing
    and a tongue for tasting
    while ten fingers do the feeling.

You might wish to add to these natural tools a watch, a magnifier, a thermometer, a pencil, paper, a ruler, and a bag to carry them in.

Now we are ready to step outside to begin our walk.

There is so much to explore in the city at each season.
    Down underfoot,
    out at eye level, and
    up overhead.

Cities have busy main streets full of traffic, noise, people,

and quieter side streets just around some corners.

   This picture shows a city street in the springtime.

   What can we find that is special about spring in the city?

   How do the bushes and trees tell you that spring is here?

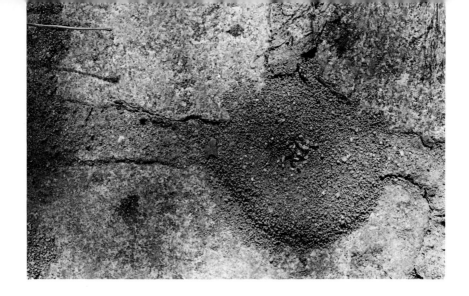

Gaze down. It all seems the same—a ground of hard gray pavement with a few cracks here and there.

But is it the same?

Look! Here, underfoot, rush a parade of ants—disappearing and reappearing in and out of a little hole, just a tiny opening in one of the sidewalk cracks.

What is all this rushing about? Where are they coming from—or going to?

To get some bread crumbs.

They don't buy bread at the store as you or I do.

Theirs is free.

Someone dropped or threw away a piece of bread, and it was discovered by an ant scout whose job it is to locate food.

The scout marks the trail in a way which ants recognize.

As news of the discovery spreads to the other ants, a rush for food begins. There are many young to feed in the tunneled-out nest below the rocky pavement.

Each ant adds to the trail marks and a definite route is established.

Lay your pencil across the trail. Do the ants go over it or around it? How long does it take for the ants to change their path?

Rub your finger across another part of the ant trail in order to remove the chemical that guides them. How do the ants react to this? How long does it take for them to be on their way again this time?

Try to tempt the ants with a new food supply. Scatter some sugar, candy, or any other bits of food and watch the ants discover it.

Lay your thermometer on the ground for two minutes. It will probably show a temperature of 70° Fahrenheit or warmer.

The ants were underground throughout the cold winter. When the weather turned warm enough they became active and cleared a passage to the outside world. Grain by grain the soil was brought up and deposited in a little pile around each opening.

These ants, like any other animals, survive wherever they can get enough food, water, air, and shelter that provides space to live and breed. Before there was a city the ants lived under rocks. Pavement is a man-made rock.

Although insects are interesting, we prefer to keep them out of our homes and out of our food. This is easily done when you know their habits.

It is not necessary to use dangerous sprays. Ants can be kept away by sprinkling some borax across their trails. Look for them on the windowsills and around doors. Covered garbage pails discourage flies. Cockroaches will avoid places that are thoroughly dry.

Look for some houseflies. What are they eating? This insect, too, finds what it needs for survival in the city, especially where there is garbage. It will lay its eggs in the filth where the young can find food after hatching. One pair of flies produces thousands of offspring in a single season.

On the most crowded of streets you might come across some large cockroaches. They were probably disturbed by some kind of construction work or repair work and fled from their dark, cozy, moist underground dwellings.

You might collect one or two of each of these insects— the ant, the fly, the cockroach. Place each kind in a separate little bottle. Then you can examine them. Since they are all insects, each has a three-part body and six legs.

Compare them according to size, color, kind of mouth, and how they behave.

You can sometimes observe a fuzzy black and brown woolly bear wandering across a city sidewalk on a bright fall day.

This caterpillar can spend the winter under a board, an old brick, or a discarded shoe. The following spring it will go through some changes and emerge as a beautiful yellow Isabella moth.

Not all city insects are found underfoot.
Look about you at eye level.
Explore the bushes and the tree trunks for insects—ants,
beetles, moths.

In the fall you might see the brown egg case of a praying mantis fastened to a twig in a bush. Although the case looks frothy, feel how hard it is. Remove the twig with the egg case attached to it. Take it home where you can watch it hatch.

Insert the twig into a moist layer of sand inside a large food jar. Fasten a piece of netting over the top. The young may hatch during the winter. Maybe two hundred predatory mantids will emerge, tiny miniatures of their large green and brown parents. They can be fed bits of meat or live insects.

You find city insects in the wintertime, too.

Overhead, in a tree, is the place to look for bagworms, among the most fascinating insects to be found in the city.

Bagworms are not worms at all, but small moths, which are seldom seen. All summer the young feed on the leaves of the tree where you find them. For protection they weave about them bags made of materials from the same tree. These coverings become portable tents.

At the end of the season each insect fastens its bag to a branch or a twig where it hangs all winter.

In the spring the immature bagworm gradually changes into an adult winged male which flies away or into a female without feet or wings.

After mating, the female lays many hundreds of yellow eggs and dies without ever having left her bag.

Winter is a good time to find and examine these bags.

If you have sharp eyes you might spy an unusual insect, such as this white tussock moth.

It came out of its leaf-wrapped cocoon.

You are sure to discover some earthworms underfoot if you explore the pavement near a patch of soil after it has rained.

How many earthworms left their burrows to come crawling out on the street?

Examine the soil area where the earthworms live. Look for little holes which are the entrances to their burrows. Count the number of holes in one square foot. By measuring the size of the area covered by soil you can estimate the approximate number of earthworms that live there.

Earthworms help to make soil loose, rich, and airy.

Birds add interest to animal life in the city. They have both wings and feet with which to move. Some take long trips, flying south in the fall and returning north in the spring. It is during these migrations that one can sometimes hear and sometimes see an unusual bird.

Your day might be brightened by the red of a cardinal, or by a handsome white-throated sparrow.

An everyday sight at all seasons in the city is the graceful soaring flight of gulls overhead. Where there are large collections of garbage, these birds gather in huge noisy flocks and become as permanent as the garbage dumps upon which they feed.

Unlike the native gulls, most city birds are immigrants. Pigeons, starlings, and English sparrows were all brought here from Europe. They found living here satisfactory and so they multiplied and multiplied. Now they are found in large numbers in all parts of our country, especially in cities where they live all year long.

These birds form groups very much the way people do. Their gathering place might be a playground, a street corner, a park bench.

What attracts these birds?

Food—any kind of nourishment. They accept garbage as readily as a dainty cookie.

Scatter on the ground a handful of leftovers from your lunch.

Soon you hear a flapping of pigeon wings and a chirping of sparrows. The birds begin to feed at once.

The pigeons walk and bob their heads. Males always seem to take time out for puffing and strutting as they court a passing female.

Sparrows chirp as they hop about and feed. The male sparrow wears a handsome black bib, unlike the plain female.

Starlings walk gracefully and silently. Male and female starlings look alike.

There are many other things to observe about these birds. Compare the numbers of each kind, their sizes and shapes, the colors of their feathers, eyes, bills.

Each of these birds causes problems in the city. The starlings become very noisy at night when they roost overhead on city buildings in huge flocks. Their droppings cover the outsides of these buildings as well as the streets below.

Pigeons, too, contribute to this kind of filth in the city.

But people love to feed pigeons. If you look carefully you will probably find some who do this regularly.

And the leftover food as well as the bird droppings attracts rats—most unloved of creatures, but a part of city animal life.

Dogs are familiar to all of us. It might be interesting to make a survey of all the dogs you meet on your walk. Note the differences in size, shape, and color. It is hard to realize that these varied animals are all related to each other and that their ancestors can be traced back to wolves.

There are not as many kinds of cats as there are dogs.

Not all city cats are house pets. In every city live thousands of wild cats that have to work for a living in order to survive.

You would not care to pet one of these cats. Neither would they encourage you to do so. In fact, they would hiss and spit if you came near them.

Nighttime is when these animals are usually found on city streets. They are busy searching for food wherever there is garbage.

These wild cats also prey on mice and rats.

Along a tree-lined street you might see some scampering squirrels and, occasionally, a horse with a policeman on its back or pulling a carriage. Horses were much more common in cities before there were automobiles.

But of all city creatures, the kind present in largest numbers is people.

A city is people and more people—living, moving, and working close together.

And as people are producing more people, the city is constantly changing to make room for them. We see more and more office buildings, school buildings, apartment houses, and shops.

Somewhere, as you walk, you may see the beginning of a new building—a hole in the ground.

This huge cavity has been gouged out of the earth with machines invented by people.

Listen to the noise that these machines make as man goes down, down, down,

> under the pavement,
> past the dark topsoil,
> past the lighter subsoil,
> down to the earth's bedrock from which soil originates.

Pick up two small pieces of rock. Rub them together. See some tiny particles flake off.

Soil consists of such grains of crumbled rock mixed with decayed bits of plant and animal materials.

Our food depends on soil for growth and we depend on food. Of course almost all soil in the city is covered by houses, parking lots, or pavement, and is unavailable for growing food plants.

Food has to be brought into cities as does water and most other necessities.

Look at the varieties of building materials about you. All have their beginnings in the earth—iron, steel, brick, wood, glass, aluminum.

Examine the beauty of some of the stones which are frequently used on the outsides of buildings.

Look for granite with its minerals of several colors.

Perhaps there is some polished limestone in which you can discover fossils. Once this rock was under the sea.

Look at the heights of buildings about you. The newest ones are often the tallest.

Sometimes there is barely space enough to walk between two tall buildings, or to see the sky, or a cloud, or even the sun, except as it might be reflected in the many windows.

Wherever enough sunlight can filter down to the ground below, we find plants, many different kinds, both natives and immigrants.

Long before all this concrete covered the city, there was a forest here, or a prairie or a farm.

Any break in the pavement encourages some green to grow again, especially when it is warm. Here is some foxtail grass growing from a crack. It makes a beautiful design against the brick wall.

You might also find crabgrass, plantain, and all too often, ragweed, a nuisance to hay fever sufferers.

There are also some colorful flowers such as the dandelion with its golden circle of blooms in the spring. Enjoy its fragrance, too.

When the flowers turn to fruit, feel the gray of the blow-balls, then blow the wispy parachutes away. Perhaps they will land in a bit of soil near a hydrant or in a crack where the seeds can start life anew.

Trees, too, add beauty to the streets. Only those which can tolerate polluted air and other urban conditions survive there. Many city trees are imports.

Trees are natural air conditioners because so much water evaporates from their leaves. Tie a plastic bag around a few leaves where it can be left for several minutes. Remove the bag and examine the amount of water that has collected. As water evaporates from the tree it takes up heat.

Trees absorb noise. A tree-lined street is quieter than one without trees.

NORWAY MAPLE BLOSSOMS

MAPLE POLYNOSES

LOCUST SEED PODS

SYCAMORE FRUIT

The flowers of the Norway maple are most attractive. Colorful blooms can be seen in early spring before the leaves unfold. As the fruits develop many flowers fall and decorate the pavement with a yellow-green carpet. Pick up some little blossoms and examine them with your magnifier. In the fall the maples again decorate the ground below them. At this time they drop their seed pods, which are called polynoses or keys.

Other city trees also produce flowers which produce fruits which bear seeds. The long pods of the locust tree are more easily seen in the winter. Winter is also the time to notice the dangling fruit balls of the sycamore tree.

Perhaps you can find an ailanthus tree with its bright clusters of fruit. Their rattle in the wind adds a pleasant sound to winter.

Select a street tree and estimate the number of seeds which it produces. What keeps the neighborhood from becoming a forest of these trees?

Trees face many hazards. Measure the soil area around a tree. There is little soil and not much room for water. Metal collars are placed around the bases of trees as a protection against damage caused by the urine of dogs.

Street trees have to be protected from people, too. Many are surrounded by fences.

Tree leaves produce food and food invites feeders.

Examine the trees to discover other lives, such as aphids, caterpillars, birds.

Besides natural city wonders, explore some that are man-made. There might be a beautiful building to study, or a statue, or a gate, or a fountain.

Your street might end at a bridge, a waterfront, or a park. Each place has something new, different, special.

You will want to walk again and again—on the main streets as well as on the side streets.

Now you know how you can make each venture outside an exploration filled with discoveries when you go for

A walk in the city.

PHYLLIS S. BUSCH has been involved with teaching, lecturing, and writing about various aspects of our environment all her life. She received her formal science training at Hunter College, Cornell University, and New York University, and has taught at every grade level from elementary school through graduate school. Her son Fred is an author and teacher of English at Colgate University. Her son Eric is a painter who teaches fine arts at Pennsylvania State University. Dr. Busch resides with her husband, a lawyer, in upstate New York.

MARY M. THACHER was born in New York City and grew up in northern Virginia. She lives with her husband and three children in New York City, except when living abroad in connection with her husband's work with the United Nations. A Bryn Mawr College graduate, Mrs. Thacher has been interested in nature photography for several years.